William Gay

Christ on Olympus, and other poems

William Gay

Christ on Olympus, and other poems

ISBN/EAN: 9783742875693

Manufactured in Europe, USA, Canada, Australia, Japa

Cover: Foto ©ninafisch / pixelio.de

Manufactured and distributed by brebook publishing software (www.brebook.com)

William Gay

Christ on Olympus, and other poems

PRIMROSES

THEY SHINE VPON MY TABLE THERE,
A CONSTELLATION MIMIC SWEET,
NO STARS IN HEAVEN COVLD SHINE MORE FAIR,
NOR EARTH HAS BEAVTY MORE COMPLETE;
AND ON MY TABLE THERE THEY SHINE,
AND SPEAK TO ME OF THINGS DIVINE.

IN HEAVEN AT FIRST THEY GREW AND WHEN
GOD COVLD NO FAIRER MAKE THEM, HE
DID PLANT THEM BY THE WAYS OF MEN
FOR ALL THE PVRE IN HEART TO SEE,
THAT EACH MIGHT SHINE VPON ITS STEM
AND BE A LIGHT FROM HIM TO THEM.

THEY SPEAK OF THINGS ABOVE MY VERSE,
OF THOVGHTS NO EARTHLY LANGVAGE KNOWS,
THAT LOFTIEST BARD COVLD NE'ER REHEARSE,
NOR HOLIEST PROPHET E'ER DISCLOSE,
WHICH GOD HIMSELF NO OTHER WAY
THAN BY A PRIMROSE COVLD CONVEY.

—W^M GAY.

During twelve years in Australasia I have received much kindness from many friends. To these with gratitude I dedicate this little book, and give herewith their names:

Hon. J. H. Abbott, Miss E. C. Arden, Miss M. Arden, Mr. and Mrs. A. Bayne, Miss Bayne, Mr. D. W. Bayne, Mr. G. Bearham, Mr. W. Blackwall, Mrs. Bon, Mr. R. W. Bogg, Miss Castwood, Miss Chapman, Mr. J. Clezy, Mr. A. Colquhoun, Dr. D. Colquhoun, Mr. and Mrs. G. Coutie, Rev. J. C. Coutie, Dr. and Mrs. H. O. Cowen, Dr. and Mrs. B. B. Cowen, Mrs. F. Dalgity, Miss E. Dawson, Hon. A. Deakin, Mr. W. D. C. Denovan, Mr. and Mrs. J. B. Edwards, Mr. J. G. Edwards, Mr. G. Fenwick, Mr. W. Fenwick, Mr. G. Gibb, Rev. J. and Mrs. Gibb, Mrs. J. Gibson, Mr. W. Gillies, Miss Goldstein, Miss Grant, Mr. R. Guy, Mr. and Miss Hadley, Miss Hollis, Mr. J. Nelson Jones, Miss Keith, Dr. F. H. Kenny, Mrs. Lambie, Mr. H. B. W. Lawson, Misses L. S. and A. E. Locke, Mr. and Mrs. G. Mackay, Rev. J. H. Mackay, Mr. N. McNicol, Miss Martin, Miss Michie, Mr. D. Mills, Mr. and Mrs. M. Moloney, Mr. M. J. Monkman, Rev. A. H. Moore, Prof. Morris, Mrs. M. Murphy, Mrs. W. Murray, Rev. S. J. Neill, Mrs. W. Nimmo, Mr. J. B. O'Hara, Mr. H. O'Neill, Mr. T. W. Orr, Miss A. Plover, Mr. T. H. Prichard, Mr. and Mrs. K. Ramsay, Mr. and Mrs. L. Richardson, Mr. and Mrs. J. L. Robertson, Misses M. E. and H. A. Sampson, Miss Ethel Saw, Mr. and Mrs. J. Sawers, Mrs. and Miss Shepherd, Capt. W. C. Sinclair, Rev. J. and Mrs. Gibson Smith, Rev. Dr. and Mrs. Strong, Mr. A. Sutherland, Mrs. M. Tankard, Mr. F. Tate, Mr. and Mrs. M. Walker, Mr. and Mrs. R. Walker, Mr. T. A. Watson, Miss Westropp, Mr. J. L. Woolcock.

Besides these there are one or two who have asked me not to print their names, and some also whose names I do not know. To these also my book is dedicated.

Christ on Olympus

Weary, at last in Zeus' high hall he stood;
Where all was vast magnificence of light,
And multitudinous harmony of song,
And music sweet of all sweet instruments,
And godlike speech and laughter. Pale his cheek,
Yet from his eyes there beamed a sacred light
Of mild inalienable majesty,
That shone amid the brightness round, as shine
Ethereal starbeams on the glow of morn.

Apart he stood and silent, breathing prayer;
To sudden stillness feast and song were hushed;
The gods, amazed, to eager lips denied
The lifted cup; and Zeus frowned darkly, yet
One boding instant trembled as he frowned;
And momentary awe contagious smote

The hearts of all, as when a flying cloud
With transient gloom obscures the sunlit hills.

Then he, the Christ, as the great throne of Zeus
Grew terrible with thunder and swift fire,
Spake; and to hear the angry gods were moved
By sweet compulsion of the voice that stilled
On Galilee the dark insurgent wave.
Even Zeus his wrath forbore, and his great throne,
As breaks the sun from brief eclipse of storm,
Was bright again with unperturbèd light:
And these the words that he, the Christ, did speak:

"Great Zeus, who from of old o'er gods and men
Hast reigned in Greece, by ordinance of Him
Who high o'er all is Lord most absolute,
Yet Whose chief name is Love, Him unto thee,
Before unknown, at last I now declare;
Whose purposes beneficent have thou
And these, His sacred ministers, fulfilled,
Your own dominion seeking; and Whose power
What ye have done amiss to good hath wrought,

As when a craftsman skilled transforms to use
That which another's wantonness hath marred.

"Yet come I not reproachful but in peace,
For have ye not by oracle and shrine,
By symbol, rite, procession, sacrifice,
Made man to know that he is more than dust
And raise beyond the earth his reverent eye?
Have not your altars shed through his dark soul
Their unremitting fires, till God should set
The eternal glory of His light therein?
And have not risen to you the halting prayers
That wingèd yet shall mount to God's high Heaven?

"From Him I come, O gods, that ye may know
That now hath He in fulness of the time
Himself to man revealed through me His Son—
Sole Lord of man at last Himself declared,
Father, Upholder, Comforter, and Judge,
Who claims all worship and bestows all love,
And, loving, would be worshipped but in love;
Nor but Himself hath shown, but unto man

Hath also man revealed and called him son,
Deep in his secret spirit one with Him,
As I with Him, and He with me, and all
With all commutually one, yet God
O'er all supreme; as stem and branch and leaf
Are one yet diverse, and o'er all the tree.

"Thus man, O gods, whose vows to you ascend,
Is peer of whom he worships, yet can ne'er
Unto the glories of his sonship rise,
If he receive not me whom God hath sent,
If free to know, to know doth yet refuse,
And free to mount, prefers the shameful dust.
But unto them that hear doth God make known
Of life in Him the fixed and sovereign law—
Divinest, holiest of the laws that speak
His sure and perfect Will: that none shall rise
Who humble not themselves, none reign but them
Who serve, none have who yield not freely all.
Yea, by His law doth God Himself abide,
From His own life in love gives life to all,
And even to death in me His Son descends

That man may know his immortality.

"To you likewise, O listening gods, I bear
The message glad, to you, God's mightiest sons:
Not man alone His care, but all that draws
From His sole Spirit life. To seek what joy,
What selfish joy, what wearisome delight,
Song and carouse and dalliance can afford,
Free in this lesser heaven may ye retain,
Immortal still, your vain divinity;
But if your godhood ye renounce, and leave
These heights to which no more ascends devout
The smoke of sacrifice, and be on earth
As men with men, and toil in mortal flesh,
To who shall be your neighbour helpful, kind,
And all the greatness of your powers still left
Bestowing freely to all loving ends,
Then ye at last on Death's strong wing shall mount
To God's eternal presence, and within
The immediate glory of His countenance live—
From heaven to heaven advanced, and power to power,
Through heaven relinquished, and through power renounced."

Brief silence held the throng, as when a lull
Foreboding tells the imminent thunder blast:
Then burst a noise derisive, wrathful, forth,
That shook Olympus, towering, many-ridged,
Deep to its base; while patiently the Christ
Upon the outskirt of the tumult stood,
Steadfast, serene, as when in tempest shines
A new-risen planet at the sea's wild edge.
Yet Hera joined not, nor august Apollo,
Nor swift Athena with the flaming eyes,
Nor lame Hephaistos: bright around them broke
Strange gleams confused of new, diviner light
The others saw not, intimations high
Of holy things that held them mute, with eyes
Now turned on Christ and now on Zeus their lord:
For Zeus, the first and mightiest, deepliest felt
Within his soul profound the word of God,
And silent sat, unprecedented thoughts
Of sanctity and love perplexed revolving,
Nor heard the uproar, to which at last awake:

"Peace, insolent gods, nor tempt the wrath that ill

Would fit my thoughts! Though hate and scorn inflame
Your furious hearts, yet what to me is due
Forget ye not! When rage befits, then rage
Shall first be mine. Nor what this stranger saith
In haste reject. If thou, O Ares, who
Delight'st in blood, thou Aphrodite, who,
Faithless thyself, promot'st the adulterous bed,
Thou, O Poseidon, plotting dark revenge,
And all ye gods of meaner state and power,
Naught see in him of worth, be ye rebuked
That unto me, the first, and those who next
In deity approach me, he hath brought
Truth that bewilders, light that blinds, a mien,
A presence, influence, divinity,
That reverence compels, yea, most compels
From those who most are to be reverenced.
Peace, therefore, nor with blatant voice, O gods,
Proclaim your own defect!

"What Power is that
Which from the topmost height of high Olympus
Even to the black Tartarean abyss

Hath from the first, inscrutable, unseen,
Held mightiest sway, which both of gods and men
Confounds the counsel and defeats the will,
Whose name is Fate? What if that Power hath now
Unveiled itself a God, not less in power
Than Fate, but greater far in righteousness
And love? Shall we revile His messenger?
His message spurn of amity and peace?
Here still remain, a crew of wrangling gods,
Cooped in a rebel heaven, divine in naught
Save in our dull interminable years,
All power on earth revoked, our altars dark,
Our temples desolate, our worshippers
To scoffers turned that mock the name of god?
Nay! rather than remain a worthless god
Within a sluggard, circumscribèd heaven,
Would I a slave on mortal earth become,
Would find in labour, service, sacrifice,
Even unrewarded, greater joy than here
Immortal sloth and lechery could give."

Then rose a mingled noise of praise and blame,

And towards Apollo Zeus inclined and said:
"What saith Apollo, whom in prophecy
No god in heaven excels?"

To which Apollo:
"Great Zeus, while yet he spake, this god or man,
I seemed to see a wider world than ours,
To see therein ten thousand temples stand,
Ten thousand times ten thousand voices hear
In praise uplifted to a loftier Heaven
Where dwell one only God and Christ His Son."

Then bright Athena, virgin of the gods,
Whose radiant eyes, the Christ beholding, seemed
To burn to adoration, suppliant spake:
"O Father Zeus, I know the words are true
This godlike stranger speaks: not one but struck
Me, half unwilling, on some inward ear,
And drew a swift assent, as though from one,
Another yet myself, that unawaked
Had until now unknown within me slept.
O Father Zeus, renounce this slothful heaven,

This empty show of poor divinity:
A newer reign let us on earth begin,
A humbler reign of labour and of love,
Humbler yet higher, joyfuller, diviner.—
O Father Zeus, renounce!"

Then low was heard
From out the throng a single voice that said,
"O Father Zeus, renounce!" Then silence fell,
Till with more certain voice another cried,
"Great Zeus, renounce!" Then silence fell, yet brief,
For now another and another cried,
"Renounce!" "Renounce!" till at the last, as spreads
From flaming tree to tree a forest fire,
A universal cry the throne of Zeus
Besieged.

Then from his throne imperial Zeus
Uprose majestic. Ne'er more godlike he
Than now when moved with noble reverence
He turned him to the Christ, who waiting stood,
Apart, transfigured, girt with effluent light

Of joy and love. And with deliberate voice
The great irrevocable word he spake:

"Son of almighty God! Such thou declar'st
Thyself, nor less than such couldst overcome
Olympus: unto Him Who sent thee I
Do now for all yield up the deity
Which erst He gave, and make His will our law."

Scarce had he spoken when, where late had dwelt
In bright aërial halls a race of gods,
There stood upon the cool and naked heights
A band of goodly men and women fair;
Who turned at length, and, not without a sigh,
Yet strong in hope, began to wend their way
In slow procession down the mountain side.

Sonnets

TO MY MOTHER

"Her children arise up and call her blessed."

MOTHER, who hast in heavenly places been
A radiant dweller even as long as I
Have been a wanderer 'neath this Southern sky,
And o'er these lands and every sea between
The shapes of Famine and of Death have seen
Me ever following, from where I lie
This song of love I send where thou on high
O'er Heaven's verge perchance dost listening lean.
Or if to inner glories thou art called,
Where earth no more disturbs the immortal sense,
Then in my heart my song I will enclose
And reach through death some nigher region, whence
The dearest strains my love's invention knows
Shall mount to thee where thou art high installed.

TO THE SEA

ON MY SISTER'S DEPARTURE FROM THE OLD COUNTRY

Be kind, O gusty Sea, to her who dares
To yield herself to thy inconstant surge:
Love's sweet ambassadress, alone she fares
On his high mission to thy farthest verge;
Be kind, O gusty Sea, for she is young,
Look thou with favour on her innocence,
Let not for her thy loud storm-hymn be sung,
Nor be to her a fear but a defence;
But if, O Sea, nor innocence nor youth
Can win thee from thy turbulence awhile,
Nor for a season turn thy heart to ruth,
Nor from thee charm an undeceitful smile,
May sacred love o'er-awe thy wild caprice
And cow thy churlish billows into peace.

RECONCILIATION

I saw of late one running here and there
About the world, who beat his breast and cried,

"O God, art Thou dethroned and dost Thou hide,
All impotent, in his infernal lair
Who now, meseems, Thy Godhood seeks to wear
And Thy just laws in scorn to over-ride,
Bestowing pain where joy should most abide,
And cursing Innocence with Hell's despair?"—
Then saw I later one of ordered mien,
With meekest dignity he passed along,
And said (as to a friend at his right hand),
"Foolish my cries, who ne'er of pain had seen
The heart divine,— O Lord, forgive the wrong!
Now have I suffered, and now understand."

THE EAVESDROPPER

I WALKED, said one, about a burial-place
One recent morn, and from a grave up-thrown
I saw an earth-stained heap of crumbled bone,
Which once was he who sang with power and grace.

Ah no! another said, in nought so base
Doth he survive: 'tis in those songs alone
Wherewith he made the hearts of men his own
That all that yet endures of him we trace.—
Then kindliest laughter, full of sweet content,
Around them broke (which yet they could not hear),
As he they spoke of lingered in his work
To catch their talk: as soul to body near,
Within his heavenly ambush he did lurk,
And smiling heard their sad, wise argument.

A HOMILY

In me behold a man but late grown wise,
Whose hairs are grey, as well with toil as years,
Who in my cradle dreamt of great emprise,
And in my youth did vow with blood or tears
To write my name across the world's wide page
In bold emblazonry; who thence confined
My manhood hale as in an iron cage
Of tasks and discipline, nor looked behind

On all the joys of wife and child and friend
Which I with sternest hand had thrust aside;
And who at last securely reached the end,
Yet found therein what most I craved denied,
And from a penny on a beggar spent
Than from a world's applause gained more content.

TO A FELLOW-TRAVELLER

[Alice Marion Sampson, who died at the age of twenty-three, on August 23rd, 1896, a few days after the Sonnet was written. She was remarkable for sweetness of disposition, strength of intellect, and nobility of character.]

Together, comrade, o'er the same rough way
We travel, thou and I, yet know right well
That roughest ways to faithful travellers tell
Of fairest lands beyond, wherein shall they
Have respite sweet from peril and dismay
And all the woes that ever yet befell
All who, like thee, their toiling steps compel
Through pain and darkness unto peace and day.—

Look up then, sister, from the weary path!
Methinks that yonder groves and flowers I see,
And golden light on many a grassy lea:
Look up, my sister, one short hour be brave,
For see! no hindrance more the journey hath
Than one poor ditch no wider than a grave.

THE RALLY

Dost thou again, dire Shape, in midnight's gloom,
As on my couch I draw my fearful breath,
Assail me with thy terrors, and entomb
Me in the blackness of thy living death,
From arid sockets urging fiery tears,
And from the midmost anguish of my heart
Forcing the rooted sighs?—But know that fears
Do I, at last arising, bid depart;
For I will face thee to thy overthrow—
From thy dark power will set my spirit free—
Once more at day a man erect will go
For all the world and God in Heaven to see,

And will, O Shadow of my ancient sin,
Again resolved, the upward path begin!

ROBERT BURNS

DIED JULY 21ST, 1796

LIKE some lone meteor from the zenith sprung
That burns with radiant sweep across the night,
A moment blazing on the startled sight
To plunge its headlong glories low among
The fatal glooms by rising tempests hung
About the wild horizon: such the height
Belovèd bard, thy spirit swift and bright
Did first enjoy, to such a doom was flung.—
But yet from where the fleeting, falling star
Of thy brief life to stormy death went down
Thy fixèd star of fame hath risen on high,
To shine with orbs that everlasting are,
And o'er the southern as the northern sky
To pour the steadfast rays of thy renown.

TO JAMES BRUNTON STEPHENS

ELDEST and first of Austral singers! Thee,
Who for thy work now tak'st of fame thy wage,
I, least and latest of thy lineage,
Do greet with reverence: yet 'twixt thee and me
'Tis not sole tie that I have dared to be
A lowly craftsman of the minstrel page,
For in thy ear and mine is still the rage
Of storms that scourge the Caledonian sea.—
Nor kin through these alone, nor that we are
Of one august dominion, yet to rise,
Even now enfranchised; but of kindred most,
That not removed from my scant youth more far
Than from thy opulent age, the Ocean lies
That frets for ever Time's unstable coast.

A SONNET OF FAITH

I AM not daunted by the show of things,
Nor do I pass them with averted eyes,

Feigning I do not see, nor on the wings
Of fair deluding fancy lightly rise
And from afar the radiant world behold
In happy silence spinning smoothly by.—
Nay, but by night and day, in heat and cold,
Among the multitudes who toil and die
I come and go observant, near at hand,
Regarding Life with eyes that do not shrink:
I see the victor on his carrion stand,
And see in impious blood the vanquished sink,
Yea, even behold where waits the delvèd sod,
Yet sing unfaltering of the soul and God.

IO TRIUMPHE!

I HAD a mirror brought to me to-day,
Wherein I scanned for long what there appeared—
The haggard lines and hues of slow decay,
The hollow cheek, the thin, dishevelled beard,
The sunken weary eye, the pillowed head—
Then looked beyond and saw, where all was stilled,

The faithful mourning ones by death's white bed,
And still beyond, and saw a grave new filled:
Then had I brought to me a pen, and wrote
Of man immortal, free, and uncreate,
In whose wide realm is death but as a mote
In heaven's great sunshine, and whom hostile fate
No more from heights eternal can debar
Than petulant winds can bind the morning star.

SUB SPECIE ÆTERNITATIS

I ASK not, Lord, to have in some far heaven
Thy recompense for ills I now endure,
For earthly pains I seek not heavenly cure,
Nor pray that unto me the crown be given
That waits ('tis said) all who with wrong have striven;
For well, O Lord, my soul doth me assure
That Thou in skill and love art none so poor
That thus to mar and mend Thy hand is driven.—
But I would ask to be uplifted, whence,
As with an angel's sight, I may behold

The plan eternal of Thy works unrolled,
View all things naked of the veil of sense,
And see in death and hunger, pain and cold,
Thy wisdom, Lord, that needs no recompense.

THE GREAT EPIPHANY

I AM the Lord: My well-beloved son
Is man; who, spirit of My Spirit, yet
Did know Me not. So therefore I did set
The heavenly orbs their course of light to run
Athwart the empty night; from chaos won
The stable earth, the surging seas that fret
The girdling coasts, the aspiring mountains met
In middle air by stooping clouds: which done,
Man out of spirit into flesh was born;
And he, I hindering not, then forth did call
The various show of city, temple, throne,
Of nations, councils, wars, feasts, ships, herds, corn:
Then I, the Lord, raised high in midst of all,
Myself upon a cross to man made known.

THE SINGER

NAY! sing no more thy wild delusive strain
(I heard them say, while I my song pursued),
'Tis but the rage of thy delirious brain
(I heard them say, yet still my song renewed);
Nay! sing no more with reckless, idle breath
Of man immortal and of life to come,
For one brief moment scan the face of death,
Then be thy foolish song for ever dumb;
Behold the dusty ash that once was fire,
And mark the summer leaf in autumn fall,
Watch thou the wavering breath of man expire,
And know that Death hath lordship over all
(I heard them say with many a scornful word,
Yet still sang on as one who nothing heard).

AUSTRALIA INFELIX

How long, O Lord, shall this, my country, be
A nation of the dead? How long shall they

Who seek their own and live but for the day,
My country hinder from her destiny?
Around me, Lord, I seem again to see
That ancient valley where the dry bones lay,
And 'tis in vain that long I wait and pray
To see them rise to men resolved and free.
Yet sure, O Lord, upon this land of death
At last Thy Spirit will descend with power;
And Thou wilt kindle patriots with Thy breath,
Who, venturing all to win their country's good,
Shall toil and suffer for the sacred hour
That brings the fulness of her nationhood.

Miscellaneous Verse

THE WAR OF THE GHOSTS

I

THREE Ghosts that haunt me have I,
  Three Ghosts in my soul that fight,
Three grandsire Ghosts in my soul,
  That haunt me by day and by night.

II

The first was a dark mountaineer,
  Who hunted with arrow and knife,
To whom the turf was a bed,
  And the wind of the moorland was life.

And the next was a mariner rude,
  Whose home and whose grave was the sea,
For whom the land was a prison
  And only the ocean was free.

And the last was a shrunken recluse,
  Who lived with the dust and the gloom,
And wrote of the Saints and of Him
  Who went for us to His doom.

III

And all through the days and years
  These ancient Ghosts contend,
And my soul is a battle-field
  Of passions that pierce and rend.

And whenever a sunbeam alights
  All gleaming and fresh on my page,
I am wild for the hills and the bush,
  I am torn with the hunter's rage.

I am sick of the smell of a book,
  I am off with the dogs or a gun,
Or I gallop my fifty miles
  Before the set of the sun.

And yet from some loftier peak
  When I catch the scent of the wave,
When I look on the sea from afar,
  I feel like one in a grave;

And I long for a ship full-sailed
  And an ocean wide on the lee—
I choke on the solid land
  For the lift of the undulant sea.

IV

Yet ever the battle goes on,
  And ever there rises a day
When the Ghosts of the wave and the wood
  To the Ghost of the cell give way.

Then the land is a wilderness drear,
  And dismal and vast is the sea,
But cloistered in peace with my books
  My soul is uplifted and free.

V

Three Ghosts that haunt me have I,
  Three Ghosts in my soul that fight,
Three grandsire Ghosts in my soul,
  That haunt me by day and by night.

Yet ofttimes there joins in the fray
  One gross and sluggish of limb,
No spectre is he but a man,
  Whose strokes are heavy and grim.

For a man is not nothing, I swear,
  Nor a braggart am I when I boast
That though he be slothful or sleep,
  A man is more than a ghost.

And my soul is my own, I aver,
  The master and lord of it I,
And whenever I will to bestir,
  All ghostly usurpers shall fly.

Then I what is mine will assume,
  Nor diverge from the path of my will,
Though the Ghosts I have routed still call
  From the desk and the sea and the hill.

THE PURSUIT

O, Love for long did fly from me,
  And I did flee from Death—
"O Love, I burn, I die for thee!"
  I cried with anguished breath.

"O Death, I fear thy dark pursuit!
  O Love, I burn, I die!
O Death, withhold thy evil foot!
  O Love, no longer fly!"

Then Love no longer fled, but turned
  And stabbed me through and through;
And Death, whom I with fear had spurned,
  My pains did all subdue.

THE VOYAGE

DRIVE on, my ship, before the blast!
  Rave on, wild sea, I fear thee not!
My sails are reefed, and stout the mast,
  And good whate'er the gods allot.

Mount up, ye threatening waves, and mix
  Your darkness with the darkened skies!
Engulf thé stars my course that fix!
  My soul your terrors all defies.

Ye hungry rocks that bellow near,
  Ye maniac winds that menace shriek,
Ye cannot strike my heart with fear,
  Nor stay me from the port I seek!

Where I shall land on any shore,
  'Tis thither joyful I repair;
Or if I sink 'neath ocean's roar,
  The heavenly port I seek is there.

THE ROPE

A Man hung down by a rope from Heaven:
  Below him was Hell
With its writhing souls; and his heart was glad
  That with him it was well;

For the rope was good, and from Heaven it hung;
  And he prayed that strength
Might be given to him ere long to climb
  Its arduous length.

Then an Angel appeared with a flaming sword,
  And bade him hope;
For he came, he said, by the will of God
  To sever the rope.

But the Man to his rope the tightlier clung,
  And besought with tears;
But the Angel upraised the flaming sword,
  Nor regarded his fears.

Then he struck with might; and exultant Hell
  Heard the Man's wild cry;
But straightway he mounted to God, Who said:
  "Thy rope am I."

A SEA MAIDEN

HER tresses are as golden bright
  As yellow sands that catch the sun,
Her lips are rosy as the light
  That dyes the wave when night is done.

Her skin is like the white sea-foam,
  Her eyes are like the morning star,
Her smile is like the lights of home
  To weary voyagers from afar.

Her breath in sweets doth more abound
  Than fragrant equatorial gales,
Her voice is pleasant as the sound
  Of rising winds in idle sails.

Like white sea-birds her thoughts do fly,
  And sweet and calm and pure is she
As April moons that imaged lie
  Within the unimpassioned sea.

THE PICTURE

THAT saint's face there, that seems as though the eyes
Saw straight to Heaven, as though, if you could look
Deep into them, you'd see reflected there
God's very glory? 'Tis by one long dead:
In youth he wrought at it for many a day;
But ever foiled by some divine ideal
He could not wholly capture, he at length
Forbore the quest. To years he lived, and grew
In artist skill, in nobleness of soul,
And all men's love, until, for friendship's sake,
He came one day to lie upon the bed
Of death. Then calling for this picture, he
With one stroke, so, and with another, so,
And so, and so, upon the unfinished face
Drew forth the look you see, and shortly died.

www.ingramcontent.com/pod-product-compliance
Lightning Source LLC
Chambersburg PA
CBHW032143080426
42733CB00008B/1181

* 9 7 8 3 7 4 2 8 7 5 6 9 3 *